All Scripture references taken from the KJV of the Holy Bible, unless otherwise indicated.

For The Sake of the Gospel: *The Fold* **Book 5** by Dr. Marlene Miles

Freshwater Press, 2023

ISBN: 978-1-960150-94-3

Paperback Version

Copyright 2023, Dr. Marlene Miles

All rights reserved. No part of this book may be reproduced, distributed or transmitted by any means or in any means including photocopying, recording or other electronic or mechanical methods without prior written permission of the publisher except in the case of brief publications or critical reviews.

Table of Contents

For The Sake of The Gospel 5

House 7

Brothers & Sisters 11

Father and Mother 13

Spouse 15

Children 17

Lands 19

Jesus Left It All 23

Do It Not! 27

There Is No Virgin Mary 28

With Persecutions 31

But You Will Go *Through* 36

Cheerful and Generous 42

Will It Be *Received*? 44

Good Grief! 46

Grieving the Purchase 50

Seeds Are Automatic 54

Excellence of Spirit 58

Spirit and Life 61

Right Spiritual Hookup 65

Prove It 68

Divine Multiplication 71

The Corporate Return	75
Godliness & Holiness	79
Fasting	82
Good Works	85
What Happened to My Seed?	89
Good News	93
Other books by this author	95
Dear Reader	100

For the Sake of the Gospel

Freshwater Press

USA

For The Sake of The Gospel

And Jesus answered and said, verily I say unto you. There is no man that have left house, or brethren, or sisters, or father or mother or wife, or children, or lands for my sake in the gospels. But he shall receive an hundredfold now, in this time houses, brethren and sisters and mothers and children and lands with persecutions, and in the world to come, eternal life,

(Mark 10:29-30).

If you have heard God's voice calling you and you've had to walk away from houses, brothers, sisters, father or mother, wife, husband, children, or land, then according to the above Scripture, you automatically should be in the 100-fold return on your financial sowing.

Adding that to all you've learned in the book series, **The Fold**, you should have no problem becoming a successful and **wealthy** Christian, blessed, and favored by God. You should not be doing without; you should not want, and you should not be depending on miracle money or handouts.

Insufficiency should not come up in your life providing you are doing profitable things, and **not** doing *un*profitable things.

What does leaving any and all of that mean?

House

Leaving your house means that you have left your natural living place, the edifice itself, but also the town, city, or community that you have lived in, come to love, and have probably found comfortable. And, you've pulled up stakes at the Lord's command, for the sake of the Gospel.

Conversely, if you have not left the house or any houses, then you may find that you are in the zero-fold return in your financial sowing if you're still stuck up under your momma and daddy. If you haven't left home, what do you need a 100-fold return *for*? Your folks can just keep taking care of you, rolling you around in a shopping cart at Walmart, getting you whatever you want as you tear down store displays. God doesn't need to pay you for executing His authority in the Earth because you're not yet doing it. Whether it's because you're too young, irresponsible, or disobedient, you're just not doing it.

God commands the blessing on us where He says we are to be, according to His riches in Glory, not according to your parent's riches in glory.

And He said unto him, **I am the Lord that bought the out of Ur of the Chaldees to give thee this land to inherit it,** (Genesis 15:7).

God has called many great men out of the land of their nativity. Abraham had to get out of the land of his birth, Ur, to fulfill destiny.

Joseph, even though he was forced to leave because of his brothers' selling him into slavery, made something of himself in the country that was not his native land. Daniel, and also Esther, were each Jews in Babylon. Daniel became a Prime Minister and Esther became a queen, respectively.

But Jesus could do no mighty works in Nazareth because they did not believe; they were too familiar with Him. Jesus wasn't wrong by being there, the people were too familiar. When God calls you out of your hometown, count it as joy. He's setting you up for 100-fold status in your financial sowing. God calls you out, He sends you, and where He sends you, He gives authority, purpose, and provision. Most notable Bible figures moved around and were *sent* by God. Being sent sets you under and in authority, and that is very profitable.

You may say and believe that our God is very peaceful. He is Yahweh Shalom, but He loves people who conquer the enemies of God, taking victory in the name of the Lord. The Lord is a mighty warrior; the Lord is His name, (Exodus 15:3). God called or sent Jesus out of Heaven to conquer. Jesus said that He didn't have a place to lay His head, that is a house, so we know He was called out, *sent*.

And Jesus saith unto them, the foxes have holes, and the birds of the air have nests; but the Son of man hath not where to lay his head, (Matt 1:20)

What fold of increase do you think Jesus had in His financial sowing, as a man on the Earth? Jesus could sow anything and reap 100-fold. The words He spoke were Spirit and they are Life. God's Word does not return void; Jesus, the Word, spoke the Word, so His results were always stellar. We should aspire to reach that level.

Brothers & Sisters

Have you had to leave brothers and sisters? I group siblings together because there is no gender in God. Our natural brothers and sisters are chosen for us. We have no say so in who they are, or who we get. Our parents' covenant is what creates and chooses our brothers and sisters, and God chooses our natural mother and father. When the Word of the Lord comes to you for salvation, what becomes of your natural brothers and sisters if *they* do not accept salvation?

When you were called to holiness and a closer relationship with God, what becomes of your brothers and your sisters, then?

They are still your brothers and sisters, in the natural, that will never change. But spiritually, if you accept a calling that they do not accept--, usually salvation, your family changes spiritually. Foremost you get a new father, which means you get new brothers and new sisters. Who are they? Any who will do the will of your Father (Mark 3:33, 3:5). Also, when you accept conversion and walk daily in holiness, but they don't, your family changes again. Many are *called* but few are chosen. Many are saved, but who will do the Will of Him who sent us?

Being born into His Kingdom, it's easy to get 100-fold new brothers and sisters.

Father and Mother

> If any man come to me, and hate not his father, and mother, and wife, and children, and brethren, and sisters, yea, and his own life also, he cannot be my disciple, (Luke 14:26)

Walking away from a natural mother and father for the sake of the Gospel can be difficult, but we are all expected to leave home at some time or other, as we become adults. If father and or mother are not doing the will of God and have no plans to do the will of God, you may have to separate yourself from them. However, for the sake of the Gospel is the key in this book because sometimes that leaving home is not just down the street or even across the state, sometimes it is across the country, the continent, or the globe.

As said, you have to physically leave them when you're called to go share the Gospel, the Good News, with the next town, country, or even the world. Either way, spiritually separated from them or physically separated from family can still hurt. But obey God. This sets the right order in your love relationships, and it prospers your soul. A prospered soul prospers a person in both health and finances, (3John 2).

This boils down to are you willing to walk away from relationships when God tells you to? Are you willing to break unholy alliances and ungodly, non-soul-prospering friendships as necessary, and at God's direction? Then you are candidate for the 100-fold level of blessings. If not, that might explain why you aren't realizing anywhere near what you could be getting in your financial sowing.

Spouse

First of all, if you are making jokes about how it will be nice to leave your spouse for the sake of a Gospel, then that is in very poor taste and no wonder you're not in the 100-fold of blessings. With that kind of attitude, God is not likely to call you or send you anywhere.

We know that the Bible is written by men and supposedly for men, but God is no respecter of persons. So, if for the sake of the Gospel, you have to leave your wife or husband at home while you go study, worship, go on missionary trips because they can't go--, it's too dangerous, or responsibilities at home won't allow them to leave, that is understandable. But if they just don't want to go, then that's on them. God will honor what you have to do, and He will provide financially.

Three men in the New Testament when Jesus called them to follow Him gave three different responses that are examples of what not to do. One man said he couldn't because he just got married, (Luke 14:20). The second man said he had to go bury his father, (Luke 9:59). In another account, the third was a rich man who was told to go sell his stuff and give the money to the poor; that man did not because he could not let go of his material holdings, (Matthew 19:16).

Well…

If you worship your spouse, brother, sister, or parent more than you love God, refusing or denying God to please them, then that could be one of the reasons why you may not be in the 100-fold return in offerings.

Children

Children are a biggie. Let's look at Abraham again. What did he have to do concerning children? Ishmael--, sent him away. Isaac? Be prepared to offer him as a sacrifice. God knows how much we love our children and how we have to be very careful not to put them ahead of God. They must be disciplined and brought up properly in the fear and the admonition of the Lord. Children should not be worshipped. That's what those examples were about.

But if you have to leave your children for the sake of ministry, for the sake of the Gospel, that is heart-wrenching, but it automatically puts you in the 100-fold return category. Here, *leave* does not mean just while you travel overnight or for a week at a time.

And this also means if your children are not doing right and just won't do right, if God says leave them alone for a season or two, then cut them off. Tough love. Whatever God says, do it. If your child's behavior or lack of it is influencing or interfering with your ministry, and they won't receive admonition, correction, or discipline, for the sake of the Gospel, cut them off.

Lands

If you have had to walk away from lands for the sake of the Gospel, then you are due a wonderful return in this lifetime. You don't have to wait for the by and by. In this lifetime means that God expects Christians, especially those who tarry in the Word and minister to others, to be prosperous 100 times in this lifetime. This means wanting nothing. It means not having to do without any good thing.

But as the Scripture says, you receive 100-fold of what you have had to sell and/or leave, for the sake of the Gospel. That means, houses, family, children, and land. But once you're in the 100-fold, you're in it so, sow!

And it is for the sake of the Gospel. If you have accepted salvation, embraced

Christianity, then you must risk losing friends by witnessing to them. If being honest is a risk, it seems the world is upside down. You must be honest with love and tell folk the truth.

I'm I my brother's keeper?

Yes, you are. Ministering to your brother is the closest you can come to as unto the Lord. If you're watching your brother slowly die and go to hell, never saying a word because you don't want to hurt his feelings or alienate him, then you haven't done anything for the sake of the Gospel. Behaviors for the sake of your brother and his feelings, do not benefit anyone in the long run. It seems you've only accepted salvation just to cover your own hind parts, especially if you are still living the way you used to live before you got saved. Your brother is your one another ministry. Your brother or sister is your foremost concern, unless God has told you to say nothing to them.

Keep sowing and getting nothing in return long enough because of your brother's or sister's slack behavior. Keep pleasing your brother or sister instead of being honest and forthright for the sake of the Gospel. Or one day decide to walk up to your brother and truly witness to him. Love him enough to care about his soul, his eternal destruction and destination. And even though this wasn't your purpose or motivation, just watch your abundant harvest come.

That is an important point, if you are doing any of the things in this book or ***The Fold*** series to **make** money come to you, and that is your motive, you are missing God. All these things are added unto you when you do what God instructs, especially for the sake of the Gospel.

As long as your backslidden sin- ridden brother sees how saved and **poor** you are, he may never ask you about God or listen to anything you have to say about God. But after you honestly witness to him, or cut him off if necessary, as you walk this thing out, you and your brother will see your harvest begin to multiply. And that's how you'll get that fish's attention.

Am I saying that an unholy alliance will affect your Prosperity? Yes. In my book, **Among Some Thieves**, I talk about borrowing, lending, and making money contracts with unsaved folk and how it drains your Grace. The unsaved who are in cahoots with you may be sponging off your Grace, doing fine, while you suffer. Better seek God on this.

Jesus Left It All

Jesus left all of that for us--, mother, Father, houses, lands, et cetera, all for the sake of the Gospel. Jesus IS the Gospel, He was spoken of, announced all through the Old Testament. Then He came as the Word to fulfill all prophecy and to fulfill the Law, ushering in the Dispensation of Grace. Thank You, Lord.

Jesus came from Heaven to Earth; He left Home. He says that in His Father's house there are many mansions; Jesus left houses in Heaven.

Jesus left His Father so that we could be grafted in, adopted by Abba.

On Earth, Jesus was born away from home. By the time He was two years old, He had to leave home again, for the sake of the Gospel. There are many thoughts on where Jesus was until He was baptized by John the Baptist but suffice it to say that Jesus went about teaching and preaching throughout the area. He taught His Disciples and also taught and healed the multitudes that followed after and sought after Him.

Jesus was on foot, else when He re-entered Jerusalem for the Passion, He would not have had to send the Disciples for a donkey that had never been sat upon. A donkey? Yes; it fulfilled prophecy. It also proves that young ones who have never heard the Gospel, can serve God. Proving that even a donkey, or those known to be stubborn, can serve God.

Jesus did not acquire real estate--, a house and lands while He was here on Earth, that we know of. He told His Disciples not to take a coat or script (money) when they go about doing ministry. In this way, Jesus left land and houses that He no doubt could have had.

Jesus was doing the work of the One who sent Him when Disciples said your mother and your brothers want to speak to you. But he replied to the man who told him, *"Who is my mother, and who are my brothers?"* And stretching out His hand toward his disciples, He said, *"Here are my mother and my brothers! For whoever does the will of my Father in heaven is my brother and sister and mother."* (Matthew 12:48-50 ESV)., Again, this shows that for the sake of the Gospel your family sometimes must and will change.

In that, I'm thankful to see that there appeared to be no household witches in Jesus' family; His mother and brothers really did serve God.

Of course, it was the plan of God that Judas would betray the Lord, but Judas was not Jesus' "blood" relative. Some, many today cannot say the same. Household witches unfortunately abound. This shows us that we all need to seek the Holy Spirit to know who is for us and who is not, and govern ourselves accordingly.

Be fruitful and multiply is one of the first things that God told man to do. That means get married. So many people are disobeying God in that wise since time began. Jesus' Earth ministry was short, so He did not marry in the natural. In a sense, He *left* spouse and children because He left off doing that in the natural. However, we know that the Church is to be the Bride of Christ, so He was saving Himself for us.

Jesus knew that on that Cross that He would lose connection with the Father because of taking on the sin of the world. He had to take on that sin, to take it off of us. He took that sin and went to Hell so we don't have to. In Hell, He took captivity captive, so we don't have to be captives in Hell, now or in eternity. Again, He left His Father, for the sake of the Gospel.

Do It Not!

Gracious Lord, on the Cross, left His mother again, ***"Behold, thy mother,"*** He said to one of His Disciples, (John 19:27). That was His way of saying, Look after her. Mary would have been in her late 40's, and possibly still vibrant. Mary's husband, Joseph, would have been close to 60, if he was still alive. Mary had 4 or 5 other children, but Jesus spoke, and this is where He wanted His mother to live.

Jesus left *things and stuff*, over and again. He wore this world very loosely. He was not trapped by the trappings of the world. Things and stuff were the very things that Satan was trying to tempt, trap and trick Jesus with, in the Wilderness Temptation after He was baptized by John the Baptist.

What "fold" of returns on sowing do you think Jesus enjoyed? Exactly.

There Is No Virgin Mary

Jesus showed His love for all, especially His Earth Mother.

None of this means that we worship Jesus' Earth mother; she was human like the rest of us. Mary did not die on the Cross, Mary did not take our sins, Mary did not descend into Hell to take captivity captive, Mary did not resurrect.

After Jesus, Mary had four or five other children--, even if she had C-sections, which she didn't she is still not a virgin. What fantasy has been given to approximately 1.3 billion people on this Earth?

The one known today and is still garnering worship as the Virgin Mary is really the Queen of Heaven. All who believe otherwise, are fully deceived. The Queen of Heaven is probably responsible for most of the people in Hell being in Hell right now. Because of the strong deception, strong ministry and anointing is needed to break the spell over those who believe that the Virgin Mary should be worshipped or that she exists, hears, answers and grants people's wishes, and prayers.

Once the Queen of Heaven gives you anything you ask for, you are on the hook, that is, in covenant with her, and on the way the Hell. The spell must be broken so that those who are deceived can be saved, worship the True Lord Jesus, and Jesus alone and not be damned to Hell while thinking they are on the way to Heaven.

Do not worship or get into an evil covenant with the Queen of Heaven. She is "queen" of the second heaven and is purported to be the wife of Satan. See that you do it not!

Jesus often said how we are to serve God--, with ALL, all of our hearts, souls, all of our mind and strength, this is the first commandment, (Mark 12:30). If we are using **ALL** toward God, there is no room for idolatry. Recall idolatry is #1 on God's most hated things list. Do it not!

Catholicism is full of idolatry and pagan worship. The "saints" that they serve so well and have even carved idols and jewelry to are renamed pagan *gods* of Africa. See that you do it not!

Catholics seem to love worshipping angels. See that you do it not!

Wake up! Jesus came from Heaven to Earth so that you could live and not die.

With Persecutions

Jesus certainly had His share of persecution. Many of us may have experienced persecution, as well. The things of God and the Gospel are foolishness to those who do not believe and are perishing. For that reason, and others, there will be mockers, scorners, and persecutors. That is built in, but at the same time you will be in the 100-fold of blessings from the Lord.

The blessings of the Lord maketh rich, and He adds no sorrow with it. God is not adding sorrow, but the world is full of sorrow. This is why there is prayer and spiritual warfare. As God is teaching our hands to war and our fingers to fight, we are able to ascend in the things of God and maintain the promotions we receive in the spiritual and in the natural. We don't marvel that demons are subject to us, but they are. Instead, Jesus said marvel that your name is written in the Lamb's Book of Life. Therefore, we also do not marvel that we are in the 30-, 60-, or even the 100-fold of returns in offerings because it is more needful and important that our names are in the Lord's Book of Life.

We'd all enjoy one hundred-fold on everything we give. However, the reason we may not have that is because some of the stuff we are sowing, we don't want returned to us: bitterness, unforgiveness, hatred, jealousy--, works of the flesh. Sowing is not just what we put in the church envelope on Sunday. We sow all day, and all night. What we are dishing out to others in kind deeds or bad attitudes will multiply and return to us if multiplication is turned ON.

All the ways of a man are clean in his own eyes, so without the Holy Spirit and one another ministry sometimes we can't even see our *stuff*.

So, as in the Garden at Eden, once Adam and Eve sinned, God immediately turned OFF multiplication. And, people of God, that is MERCY.

As you are now seeing that rising to the receive high returns in offerings is a **lifestyle**, it is based on the way you live 24/7, and not just the way you are on Sunday at offering time. It is not based on how much you sow, so getting in the $1000 line, or the $100,000 line makes no difference if you are not living right before the Lord.

- Lord, let the minister who regularly calls for a certain amount to be sowed in the offering hear from You before he or she opens their mouth to ever say that again, in the Name of Jesus. Amen.

It is not based on need, either, because if any of us are in the flesh we have needs, because God is not blessing our *idols*.

What idols?

The idols in our souls that impart their nature to us, and we are acting out what the idols want us to do in the natural. *Such as?* Fornication, adultery, pride, anger. Yeah, all the works of the flesh. God is not prospering that. God will not give you financial increase to finance your evil. Unless you are saved, and have the Holy Spirit, you cannot see your own filthy rags, or outright nakedness, for that matter. Neither could the Church of Laodicea.

It is not how we look on Sunday, at church or in the company of the Pastor or other good, saved folks. It is who we really are when no one is looking. We should have on Jesus' Righteousness, not our own:

> We are all infected and impure with sin. When we display our righteous deeds, they are nothing but filthy rags. Like autumn leaves, we wither and fall, and our sins sweep us away like the wind, (Isaiah 64:5)

God is Spirit and He is Truth. By being saved, when God looks at us, He sees Jesus, that is if we have on Jesus. If God looks and sees idols – He is not blessing that. We all have to do better and by salvation, and practicing the Disciplines of the Faith and the Holy Spirit we can all do better, if not for ourselves, for the sake of the Gospel. Christians and sinners are looking.

> For they being ignorant of God's righteousness, and going about to establish their own righteousness, have not submitted themselves unto the righteousness of God,
> (Romans 10:3).

But You Will Go *Through*

Make no mistake you have left people and houses and land for the sake of the Gospel. But also for the sake of the Gospel you will go *through*. Every great in the Bible went through something, it was part of what made them great. Life, whether you are saved or not, is not necessarily going to be a bowl full of cherries. Everyone goes through something, unless you have a perfect ancestral foundation and you never sin. Okay, that's impossible, but if you're saved, *that* you're saved gives you help from Heaven. It gives you protection and hope that the troubles of life will not overtake or destroy you.

Those who appear to be living a charmed life, might just be living a **charmed** life. It is better to live a life in Christ now, go *through*, and remain in Christ in your living, so in eternity, you do not have to pay in Hell.

The Disciples left to follow Jesus. After Jesus' resurrection they ministered as they had been commissioned. Some were apprehended, imprisoned, beat down, persecuted.

God's purpose, I believe in putting anyone in the 100-fold of returns in the sowing of a *sent one* is not necessarily so they can live a cushy life, but it is so they do not spend their days and nights **thinking about money,** needs, stuff, and provisions. That is earthly, fleshly stuff. Thinking of money all the time is worshipping Mammon, whether that was the person's intention or not; it was Mammon's goal.

The thoughts and prayers of a *sent one,* a minister and preacher of the Gospel should be on the things of God, not the things of this world. Therefore 100-fold, 60-fold, 30-fold return in giving is liberating. It liberates the person from the flesh life, freeing him or her to flow into the spiritual, giving time and attention to prayers, fasting, praise, worship, and ministering to others.

Therefore, be assured that you can and should obey God and do the purpose you were sent here to do. Further, know that God is always with you; Jehovah Jireh will provide. Leave off worrying about and thinking about the small things of this life, greater things you should be doing, greater things you should be attending to, and greater things you should aspire to, in the Name of Jesus. God promises the true riches and that is the spiritual things, not money, silver, gold, and Bitcoin.

Money, things, and stuff is not a goal, unless those are your *idols*. Your eyes should be on God and **all things** necessary for life and godliness will be added to you.

Knowing that you are in 100-fold return on offerings should give you comfort and be assurance that whatever you ask God for, especially for His people, He will give it to you in abundance so there will never be lack in your life or ministry. Listen, even if your ministry is at your own house--, it's just your spouse and kids, you still have enough, even abundance.

Those with a larger mandate and a bigger mantle whose calling is to more than just four people, you are also in the 100-fold so whatever you need for your ministry, purpose, destiny, and legacy will be given in great abundance.

While you are yet praying, God is answering and His answers are always yes, and Amen.

Some historical accounts of what may have happened to the Disciples of Jesus follow. Surely, nothing as heinous will happen to you, but these men were willing to lay down their lives to see that the Gospel was spread abroad to Jerusalem, Judea, and the uttermost parts of the Earth. Compared to where they lived, most of us live in the uttermost parts of the Earth, so we should be eternally grateful to God and these great ministers of the Gospel.

The Disciples, who became Apostles ministered for years, but in old age they still were hated and died grievous deaths. Some were crucified, hung, skinned alive, crucified upside down, beheaded, stabbed, run through with a sword, thrown from a high place, survived the fall, then was beat to death with clubs. Another stoned, then bashed with a club in the head. Another was impaled with iron hooks. One was crucified and then cut in half. At least one was stoned and beheaded.

John was the only one who died a natural death, not a martyr's death. He was exiled for a time on Isle of Patmos but then released and preached in Turkey until he was 100 years old. Matthew was staked and speared to the ground. Peter was crucified upside down at his request. Mark was dragged to death.

The point of all of this gore is to show how evil and barbaric the people were in that time. Also, it shows that the territorial and political demons (idol *gods*) incited the people greatly and to do great evil. You can see how evil these demons are and how they do not want the Word of God preached. You can see how deceived the people of that time were into polytheism and idolatry. You can see how desperately people needed Jesus, and the Word of Truth. And you can see that the world still needs the Gospel preached, else they would all be perishing and bound for hell.

Whatever demons are allowed into the heart of a man is wicked, so wicked; this is why God said the heart of man is wicked. An unsaved man attends to the directives of evil demons, whether he realizes it or not. The fact that he doesn't realize it is why it is so effective.

Cheerful and Generous

Give and it a shall be given unto you, good measure, pressed down and shaken together, and running over shall men given to your bosom. For with the same measure that you mete withal, it shall be measured to you again, (Luke 6:38).

After that last chapter you should rejoice that you are not being attacked by a mob for your Christian belief, or the words of Truth that come out of your mouth. For that reason and others, you should be thankful that you are in a civilized setting and are *able* to give or sow in offerings.

You should be happy that you can be a sower, and a giver. One of the most accurate measures of motive is *how* you give. This is gauged by both your emotions as you're giving as well as *how much* you give, based on what you have to give. How your emotions are as you're giving will affect how much you give. Too many times it's the other way around. How much you have to give affects your emotions and giving, especially when you have two little to give or feel that you have two little to give. Or how much you're having or being forced to give is affecting your emotions. You should never have the emotions of drudgery or discontent in sowing. If you do, then your harvest will be affected negatively by your negative emotions,

Psychologists say that it is painful for some to even pay their bills; it is painful for people to let go of money. Why? If money is their *god--*, nobody wants to let go of their idols.

Will It Be *Received*?

Remember your seed has to be *received*, but if you don't present it well, who will want to receive it? They say that a baby in the womb responds adversely to the mother who doesn't want it, even if negative words are never spoken over the child the whole nine months that she's pregnant. Surely you don't think a fully grown seed is going to run to you when it reaches fullness if you've never expressed anything positive toward it or spoken anything favorable over it.

You're expecting your seed to be received, but why are you hiding it? Why is it all balled up? Why is it folded up like so much bad origami and stuffed in an envelope? If you're not pleased to bring it, then no one is going to want to receive it. God hates a bad offering, a blemished offering. He says that it's an abomination to Him.

Conversely, a cheerful giver reflects the quality of the offering. If I have a gift, that I am pleased to present. I will be cheerful, and generous, offering that gift with honor. That's what God wants from us because that's the kind of gift that He *receives*.

Good Grief!

Many times, people get emotional when paying bills. Dread when paying bills or spending money and other emotions are not prospering you, they may be UN-prospering you. They really are not profitable to your soul, physical body, or health. Drop these superfluous emotions. Those emotions are either caused by strongholds or inviting strongholds. If you made the bill, when you receive the statement and when you write the check, buy the stamps, or go to the post office to mail those remittances, why not rejoice, praise God the whole time that you're tending to your bills?

Rather say, Lord, thank You for the new car that I'm driving. I thank You for the sense of assurance and security that I have when traveling on the road. I thank You that I can go to work efficiently and can even take weekend and recreational drives out in the country. Thank You that You are the provider of all good things in my life. I praise You that I now have a chariot that I can even pick up sinners and saints and take them to church with me. Thank You, Lord, for supplying all my needs according to Your riches in glory. Thank You for the means to take care of these expenses, in Jesus Name, Amen.

You don't have to rejoice that you are in debt, but don't lament it either. Just purpose in your heart and in your will to become debt free.

> Owe no man any thing, but to love one another: for he that loveth another hath fulfilled the law, (Romans 13:8)

There may be seasons of debt in a person's life, but we should not let lust, greed, and desperation cause us to make a habit of it. People laugh when I say of spam marketing calls, "Oh, that's someone calling to sell me money." It's really the truth. Why should

$1,000. cost you $1,100 unless someone is *selling* money? Interest is only of interest to the person selling the money. Period. Charging $300 on your credit card may cost you much more than $300 by the time it is all paid back. Credit card companies are "selling" money. When money costs money, that is added sorrow. You know for sure it is not from God if there is an upcharge to things you should easily receive.

Stop buying money from people and start *receiving* money from God.

Its the same way with a car or other high-ticket items. Financing it may cost you $5,000 over the cost of the car when it is said and done. Stay out of that trap as much as possible. But if your vehicle is financed, pay with cheerfulness, honoring your contract until you can rise to a better place financially.

In your soul, remember the joy you experienced when you saw that car, refrigerator, or whatever you purchased on time. Remember how you may have prayed to

God for it long before He led you to it, or before you ever saw it. Now, if you purchased it on credit, well, it is what it is. Do not plan to finance every car or expensive item you buy all of your life, unless you are putting it on a credit card to get extra points and then paying the credit card completely off at the end of the month.

Grieving the Purchase

If you feel you've missed God in receiving Wisdom to make the purchase, repent. You've got to get over the condemnation and stop grieving the purchase. Grieving a purchase that you have no intention of carrying back to the store, especially one with a mortgage or payment book, is foolish. What's it going to accomplish? And until you stop grieving, the pain and the hurt doesn't stop. Have you noticed that as long as you are grieving, you don't get any breakthrough or release from the bill?

As long as you are grieving you are inviting any number of evil *spirits* into your soul and as mentioned, building strongholds. Strongholds can run in families, so if you invite one, you may pass it on into your generations.

I know a young person, at 19 years old, is obsessed with getting things for free and not spending their own money. Where did they get that stronghold? The thought of spending a dime is painful to them. This person has a one year or less work history, has a paid-for car that was given to them, and lives at home still. So where would they get a stronghold against spending money?

It's generational.

I've discovered a category of shoppers that I call the shopping bulimics. They buy everything they want, almost everything they see, but when they get home, they reconsider their purchases. Sometimes they grieve their purchases. Some wait until they get their credit card bill or another bill in the mail that is higher than they thought. Then they take everything or most of it back to the store. They aren't cheaters necessarily. They haven't worn these items or done any damage to them. But like folk who have eaten too much, they feel guilty and want to throw it all back up. These shopping bulimics do the same thing when they can. When they can't, they grieve the purchase. You may have to hear about it from now to Kingdom come.

We are not our own, but we are bought with a price, and that price was the life of Jesus Christ. Aren't you glad that God is not *grieving the purchase* as it pertains to us?

Some grief is natural, but constant grief leads to depression, and the *spirit of heaviness*. That *spirit* ushers in depression. None of these evil *spirits* are conducive to you receiving 100-fold from the Offering on Sunday if you're behaving this way Monday through Saturday.

As worship is profitable to your seed, then *grief, heaviness,* and *depression* are not profitable to your financial seeds that you are sowing. This behavior belongs to those who are unprospered in their souls. You have the car and are driving it wherever you want to go, but you're griping because you have to pay for it? That is childish, selfish, immature, and ungodly. Pay your commitment. Amen.

When it comes to seed that you have sown in the Offering, you must be a cheerful giver, because grieving sown seed will kill it; don't do that. See that you do it not!

Seeds Are Automatic

What seeds, you may ask?

You may be spending everything you have and make on your new car. Then you should have grief; repent, get rid of the thing that is keeping you from obeying God. If you're robbing Him in tithes and offerings, but you have a shiny new car, well, don't come pick me up in that thing. Sell the car, get more practical, and then you'll be more profitable.

You are the planted of the Lord, and you should have seeds--, good seeds regularly, and in season. This was discussed at length in the first book of this series.

What tree doesn't automatically have seeds? Plants automatically have seeds. Some tubers and other plants sprout again from their roots. Being able to reproduce in nature is without conscious thought; it just happens. If we are the *planted* of the Lord, trees of righteousness, then we should regularly have seeds.

If you are not robbing God in tithes and offerings *and* still driving your new car, rejoice, be exceeding glad, for great is your reward. The purchase that God is allowing you to use, even if you're paying for it on time, is a blessing. Rejoice that you have a good name (reputation) and were able to get credit if you needed it in this season.

Those who are prospered in their souls have the same emotions when paying a bill as they do when sowing financial seeds in the offering. They are cheerful, happy, even rejoicing. Keeping your eyes on God will always prosper you. If you study the latest fads, or are constantly looking for something new to buy, you will surely be tempted. Next time access Wisdom from God before the purchase so that the thing you think you bought and own does not actually own you.

As we discussed earlier, your soul is very powerful, and it can affect the return in your sowing. You will want to sow, not only cheerfully, but also generously. Of course, if you are cheerful, you will be generous. If you are not cheerful you can think you're sowing $1,000,000 and expecting some amazing return from God, but it will only be giving; that is not sowing, you grouch muffins. Pay attention.

With the same measure you mete, it shall be returned back to you, (Luke 6:38). Be a generous giver, cheerful giver, sow generous offerings. Your return will come also back to you, ungrudgingly, generous and cheerful.

A generous giver is cheerful and obedient. A cheerful, generous giver is willing, and obedient.

If you are willing and obedient, you shall eat the good of the land, (Isaiah 1:19).

If you're neither willing nor obedient, you can forget that promise.

Cheerful and generous sowers are always welcomed, into the Fold, appreciated, and increased.

There is not a plant on Earth that will not let go of its seeds and let go willingly. Holding on to and harboring seeds will kill the plant and all future generations of the plant. It will lead to extinction.

Humans, what are we doing?

Excellence of Spirit

God blessed Daniel and his three Hebrew friends for their excellence of spirit. What is excellence of spirit? A meek and quiet spirit.

> Well, let it be the hidden man of the heart. And that which is not corruptible. Even the ornament of a meek and quiet spirit which is. In the sight of God of great price,
>
> (1 Peter 3:4).

An *excellent spirit* is a meek and quiet spirit. The word, *meek* translated, means *like God*. Excellence of Spirit will be evident when you habitually choose the better way rather than having to be **forced** to obey it. It is exhibiting mildness of character and humility, not self-promoting.

The word, *quiet* means all that you think it means. It also means, *still, sedentary, remaining in one's seat.* To me that means remaining in one position, not self-promoting or selfishly ambitious. That means properly set under authority, not trying to be over the authority that you should be set under.

The quiet and meek-spirited person is very valuable to God. What God values He keeps, protects, blesses, and shows favor to. And He rewards that. God connects with this type of person because of that. When this type of person sows, God receives their seed. A sower who sows in worship with a sense of expectancy also has a meek and quiet spirit. That person will probably reap high returns in the offering.

> He that hath knowledge spareth his words, and a man of understanding is of an excellent spirit, (Proverbs 17:27).

The Proverbs tell us that a man of understanding has an excellent spirit, that the man with an excellent spirit attends to Wisdom and understanding. He doesn't run his mouth all the time.

Jesus had a more excellent ministry, probably because of the excellence of His Spirit. The Book of Daniel speaks often of an excellent spirit, and that is the man to whom God reveals knowledge and understanding, Wisdom, hidden mysteries, and secrets. Again, we know from the Proverbs that the man who receives Wisdom is valuable in God's eyes. Whereas a fool is the opposite. Being a fool or becoming foolish is not profitable.

Spirit and Life

> It is the spirit that quickeneth the flesh, profiteth nothing. The words that I speak into you, they are spirit and they are life,
> (John 6:63).

Sowing by the unction of the Spirit toward the Spirit while in the spirit will ensure abundant returns. Being in the Spirit when you sow, and staying in the Spirit as much as it is possible while your seed is growing, is what will profit you most. That will keep you from making unprofitable moves, mistakes, and having bad responses, reactions, and outcomes.

Conversely, the flesh and its actions and responses kill spiritual seeds, choke spiritual seedlings, and destroy spiritual harvests.

That doesn't mean to come to church as often as possible while you have seed in the ground, but it does mean to come to church as often as possible. It means in your daily life, make use of spiritual knowledge even in your everyday situations.

For 100-fold return in your sowing, it is necessary that your flesh is in check, disciplined and orderly. Your sowing must be a *worship,* not just a praise, not merely a Thanksgiving, but a **worship**. Worship sowing is 100-fold sowing.

Worship cannot be an accessory. You feel sympathy for the cause, so you give under the pressure of your emotions. Emotional giving is not spiritual sowing; it is only soulish sowing.

Because the pastor said, *sow*-- that's obedience.

Or because everyone else is, then that's just giving.

Obedience is good, but there are better motives, and God looks on our motives as part of how He sees what *fold* we are sowing in.

Blessed are the poor in spirit, for theirs is the Kingdom of heaven, Matthew 5:3.

Further, considering excellence of Spirit, one of its components, meekness, is outlined in the Beatitudes. Those who are poor in spirit are meek. They're not puffed up or prideful. They're precious to God, so precious that theirs is the Kingdom of Heaven. Having the Kingdom of Heaven means that you have full inheritance, and access to all that is in it. *Full* implies 100%.

Conversely, pride and arrogance are the substance of what you *think* you are, wish you were, but deep down inside, know that you're not.

In God there is no excellence in the prideful, even though excellent is what they appear to be on the outside, prideful boasting, and bragging all go together. They are not profitable. Meek and quiet go together, and that equals excellence.

> Blessed are the meek, for they shall inherit the earth. (Matthew 5:5).

> The earth is the Lord's and the fullness thereof. Psalms 24:1.

The Earth shall yield her increase to you (Ezekiel 34:27); you shall have abundant harvest whenever you sow because the Earth is under your authority and dominion as you work spiritual seeds by sowing in the offerings.

> Blessed are the pure in heart, for they shall see God, (Matthew 5:8).

Purity of heart correlates to excellence of spirit, and proper motive. Sowing with the right motive will move the heart of God to your prosperity. Seeing God is very profitable because everywhere He steps there's prosperity. Seeing God means He manifests to you; wherever He steps, there is fullness, riches, and wealth.

Right Spiritual Hookup

But the manifestation of the spirit is given to every man to profit withal,

(1 Corinthians 12:7).

Why would the Word say that the spirit is given to every man to *profit*? As discussed earlier, the Spirit is what ministers revelation, Wisdom, understanding and knowledge to the heart, the spirit of man. That is, the Spirit ministers the Word to your spirit. The Spirit advises and counsels you in everyday life as well as your worship and sowing decisions. The Spirit will tell you when, where, and how much to sow. Or you can just guess, or do what everyone else is doing--, which is not profitable. Remember the direct correlation between Wisdom and riches from Proverbs 3.

Manifestation of God by His Spirit will cause deliverance. Where there is deliverance, there's victory over God's enemies. Where there's victory, there's spoils. Spoils show up as prosperity from your seeds. Folks who have not sown anything cannot seriously be wondering where their increase is.

Those who have fought no spiritual battles cannot seriously be wondering where their spoils are.

But God hath revealed them unto us by his spirit. For the spirit searches all things. Yea, the deep things of God,

(1 Corinthians 2:10).

The spirit of man is the candle of the Lord, searching all the inward parts of the belly,
(Proverbs 20:27).

The Spirit searches the deep things of God, then brings knowledge, revelation, and information to your spirit.

Your human spirit is trying to be a copy of the Spirit of the Lord, or it should be. It is also searching out the deep and inward things they communicate. Even if you suddenly get an idea or something comes to your mind, if it's from God, it came through your spirit man from the Spirit of God. There was no light bulb over your head turning on. There were no crib notes floating in the air to magically enter into your head. You may have seen or read a thing, but if the Spirit of God didn't quicken it to your understanding, bring it back to your remembrance, or cause it to appeal to your intellect, it just floated by.

Prove It

I'd love to prove it to you.

How many times have you read the very same passage of Scripture in the Bible but one day read a certain verse that you've read 10 times before, but that day it came alive. God quickened it for your spirit at that time, or you were finally quiet enough, which is an excellent thing for your spirit man to receive the impartation of the quickening by the Spirit of God. That day, those words came ***alive*** and jumped off the page at you. Those words taught you something, imparted something to you, guided you, or led you to an answer of a perplexing problem, or inspired your spirit man to a new level. Whenever there is a *quickening* or realization that God is present, that's a good time to sow.

Here's a good place to say that you don't have to wait for Wednesdays and Sundays to sow in the offering. If the Spirit of God quickens, that it's time for you to sow; do it right then. Call your offering into your church, or use your credit or debit card online, e-mail, PayPal, CashApp, Zelle, or whatever.

Better, bring ye the tithes and offerings into the storehouse, (Malachi 3). Jump in your car, ride to the church, and sow accordingly and obediently. Bless that seed all the way to the church. After all, it's your *son*. It has to learn and obey the sound of your voice sooner or later.

But it's not Sunday or Wednesday night who's going to bless it? You can bless it all the way to the church; Jesus blessed things before He multiplied them --, fishes, loaves, water turning into wine. Then have the pastors or day church staff members to agree with you and send up prayers as they receive the offering.

Ultimately it will get to the priests of the house for his/their blessing. But who says you have to wait for the traditional call to sow in the offering in any service? People are bringing their seeds up as the man or woman of God is preaching. Of course, this could be very distracting for the preacher, but it depends on how the service is flowing and how big the auditorium is. It also depends on who the speaker is and how many armor bearers or security people are in place. Warning, if your motive isn't pure, just don't do it.

Divine Multiplication

Similarly, who says anyone has to wait for a traditional call to be saved? If folks have to wait to be saved on Wednesdays and Sundays some folk wouldn't get saved.

Make an altar where you are and minister salvation to whomever God sends you to, or whomever asks. Take down your **CLOSED** sign because it's a *poor attitude* and minister to people wherever you are.

Excellence of spirit creates and insures a strong spiritual hook up with God. Being connected is critical in planting, growing and harvesting. If a tree is not properly connected to its soil and root system, it will not bear. If a tree or vine is not connected correctly the fruit will be non-existent or small.

Spirit-to-spirit that's how any kind of Divine Multiplication is done. If you want Multiplication in the natural you've got to have intimacy. If you want Multiplication in the spiritual, you also need intimacy. Intimacy only comes by relationship, and relationship comes by spending time with, courting and being courted.

Spirit-to-spirit sowing is how finances prosper to overflowing. Spirit-to-spirit is how God transfers information to you, as well. Spirit-to spirit; Heaven over you must be open.

Spirit-to-spirit happens in worship.

Sowing because your mind said so, you feel tingly, or your emotions are charged is out of your soul, not by the Spirit. The soul is a big part of the entire experience as you come into the Courts of the Lord, but there must be a spiritual connection. In Thanksgiving, in our mind and intellect we have sense enough to remember God and what He's done for us, and thank Him, accordingly. Enter into His courts with Praise, that's celebration; the emotions are turned on here. Bless His name.

Entering into worship requires that our spirits be quickened. It is our spirits that commune with His Spirit to quicken us (make us alive enough) to enter into the Holy of Holies. I am not saying that your mind or your emotions are bad, I'm just saying the connection that you want for 100-fold return in your offerings is spirit-to-Spirit.

When your harvest manifests, it's because God has spoken and commanded the blessing over you. The words He speaks are Spirit and they are life. When words are Spirit, you must receive and understand them by your spirit, or you won't know what God just said: When, where and how much to sow and where your harvest is, or how to receive it.

Any and every attribute of Jesus' Spirit is considered Excellent; and He tells us not to be unequally yoked, so Excellent Spirit connecting to Excellent spirit is the ideal that He is looking for. Of course, none of us are perfect, but God will honor our faith and our trying as though we are holy, imputing the Righteousness of Jesus to us. (But, we have to at least try.) Therefore, any and all character traits and spiritual components that Jesus had would make for Excellence of spirit.

And, Excellence of spirit assures the right spirit-to-Spirit hook up and God receiving your seed for abundant harvests. That's abundance, way up there, probably in the 100-fold return.

The Corporate Return

> And if they right eye offend thee, pluck it out, and cast it from thee: for it is profitable for thee that one of they members should perish, and not that thy whole body should be cast into hell.
>
> And if they right hand offend thee, cut it off, and cast it from thee: for it is profitable for thee that one of they members should perish, and not that they whole body should be cast into hell. Matthew 5:29-30

Sin is not profitable; godliness is.

If a part of your body offends you that means it was rebellious or disobedient. When it comes to offense or sin, starve the parts of your body, mind, or soul that want to do or think on things that transgress against God.

Fast. Fast food, beverages, and certain activities. If a favorite restaurant serves the most fantastic, whatever you like to eat but you know when you get there you are going to order mixed drinks; don't go there. Fast *places*, until you have full deliverance.

Don't literally cut off body parts, just stop feeding your ungodly lusts and desires. Cut off body parts by not giving them what they want. No eye candy. No liquor. No candy. No drugs, et cetera. Cold turkey doesn't work for everything and everybody but fasting (resistance) is your first line of defense. Simply put, godliness is being like God, and godliness is profitable.

God gives us all things that pertain to life, and life is what you care the most about. He also gives all things that pertain to godliness--, that's what He cares most about--, although He cares about your natural life, as well. Bodily exercise profits little: but godliness is profitable.

> Unto all things, having promise of the life that now is, and of that which is to come, (1 Timothy 4:8)

When a member of your church congregation habitually offends the Body, measures should be taken to correct the matter. Have they been gone to privately? Have they been spoken to with a witness? Have they refused to change? Have they refused help? Have they declined counseling, and or deliverance? Are they behaving as a reprobate? They are offending the *Body*.

God judges individuals, so you can't hide in a church. He also judges churches, so you can't hide in a church.

Has the pastor said, *Break fellowship* with such an individual? Are you obeying that directive? No? Well, no wonder you're broke. Are you disobeying spiritual leadership, sinning in an unholy alliance? Are you communing with an offender of the Body of Christ? Are you grieving the Holy Spirit? No wonder you're poor and broke.

Remember asking your mom for something when you were a kid, but she said, *"No not until you clean your room"*? If you're doing any or all of what is listed above, your *spiritual* room is filthy. Go clean your room!

Is the church, as a whole, obedient or disobedient? That's why the Corporate Return is the way it is.

Godliness & Holiness

They disciplined us for a little while as they thought best; but God disciplines us for our good, in order that we may share in his holiness. (Hebrews 12:10)

The Holy Spirit will bring you under conviction when sin is present. Being chastened by the Lord may not seem like too much fun, but He corrects you because He loves you. As you yield to His chastening, that leads to correction, which leads to holiness. It doesn't only lead to holiness, but to be partakers of His Holiness as well. When we partake of His Holiness, it allows <u>*us*</u> entrance into the Fold and into the Holy of Holies. Without His righteousness, we couldn't *enter in*. Folks can't sneak in. They may believe they're *in* or they may act as though they're *in,* deceiving themselves. If you don't have the manifestation of ***in*** you are not ***in.*** A manifestation of being or living in the Holy of Holies is that when you sow, you reap 100-fold.

In Bible times, if a priest who was not pure went into the Holy of Holies, he would have to be dragged out--, dead. If you were obedient, you wouldn't have needed correction. But correction is because of God's Grace toward us. Better put on some holiness. Jesus gives us His righteousness, so there is no excuse for not having any. God wants you to *enter in* so much that He helps.

When you go to a fine restaurant if you are not properly dressed, they lend you a jacket and a tie so you can *enter in*. God will give us His Holiness and His righteousness--, a whole robe of righteousness so that we can enter into His presence.

This doesn't mean that you have to walk around super-holy all day. Well, your reasonable service is expected, and your representation of the Body of Christ as well as your local church is not too much to ask. Remember, you must continue being a role model to sinners as well as a role model to your *son* (the *seed* that you've sowed in the offering on Sunday), as well as do your part corporately in your church.

Godliness and holiness are sure ways to keep you profitable.

Fasting

Blessed are ye that hunger now, for you shall be filled. Bless it are you that weep now, for you shall laugh,

(Luke 6:21).

This passage in Luke--, is where that give until it hurts thing probably came from. If you give a seed that is so huge that you have no money for food next week you will definitely be fasting. And fasting hurts. Fasting hurts many folks and demons, but that's not exactly what this verse means. Fast on purpose, not because you don't have anything to eat. And involuntary fast doesn't please God any more than you'd be pleased by an involuntary clearing of land in the back of your house because your teenager decided to see what matches could do when the adults weren't looking. Involuntary fasting is not as profitable as ***choosing*** to fast out of obedience or receiving unction to fast from the Holy Spirit. Accidental fasting or fasting because of poor planning, time, or money is about as profitable as burning down a forest by mistake.

Unholy Alliances

The mixed multitude fell a lusting, (Numbers 11:4). Not just the Israelites who left Egypt, but still, in our time. Now we live in a mixed multitude, there are both saved folk and unsaved folk, believers and unbelievers all living together. We have to choose carefully with whom we make alliances. Don't make a covenant with just anybody. Bad company corrupts good manners. Sometimes God can't bless you the way He wants to because of who you're hanging out with. Your friendships, alliances, and relationships affect how God can bless you.

Jesus saith unto them, My meat is to do the will of him that sent me, and to finish his work, (John 4:34)

For the sake of the Gospel do everything you do as unto the Lord. He will always provide.

Good Works

Good works are profitable.

This is a faithful saying, and these things I will that thou affirm constantly, that they which have believed in God might be careful to maintain good works. These things are good and profitable unto men, (Titus 3:8)

As a matter of fact, it is works on which the saved will be judged at the judgment. God is giving everyone purpose and stewardship in the Earth and the wise attend daily to their respective jobs. The lazy are not rewarded by God, and the Bible also says those who don't work should not eat. Many of the Proverbs talk about the sin of laziness and poverty, corruption and destruction that follow laziness.

Works will be judged. Only what you do for God will last, so the works will be tested and tried. Only those works that pass the trials and tests of fire will be reward worthy. Works that are not hay, wood, or stubble will remain.

Work for the sake of work and not for the higher purpose of helping others, or to glorify God is not as worthy as work backed by faith with a definite purpose in mind.

Good works are desired, but it is not as profitable as works coupled with faith, pure motives, and godliness. The Pharisees performed the rituals of religion, but they did their works to make themselves look good, not to seek God or bring glory to God. That was religion for the sake of religion. Religiosity, and fake piety will not prosper you spiritually or financially with God. Religion is a work, and it takes work because it is not of God. Works that are of God are actually good and is actually God doing the work *through you*, not you, in your flesh, doing the work.

Religious people usually come off as super holy, but they generally only want the reward, notice, and acknowledgement of people.

> Making the word of God of none effect through your tradition, which you have delivered in many such like things do ye, (Mark 7:13).

In other words, doing religious things, trying to appear godly, pious, or holy may fool some of the people some of the time, but it will not prosper seeds that you have sown in the offering. It will not sway God to cause your seed to grow to 30, 60, or 100-fold for the increase of your harvest because God is not mocked. If what you're doing has no true heart of giving, ministry, the love of God, or is about His people, it will not foster a healthy harvest in your sowing.

Neither can God be tricked by the size of your seed, the repetition of your prayers, the loudness of your praise, or the tears in your worship if it is not real.

If it is not real to you, it is not real to God.

If your Pew neighbor is pouring out a lot of attention and facial tissues to you, even if you fooled every human being in the sanctuary, God is not mocked. God cannot be deceived because He is not a liar or deceiver. There's nothing in Him that can be fooled.

A mock seed grows a weed. Mock Praise will never impress God. Mock worship will never water your seed. Mock parenting will not minister to your seed. Mock cultivation will grow nothing.

What Happened to My Seed?

If after you've sown seed, your harvest doesn't manifest or manifest in the expected way, increasing 30-, 60-, or 100-fold, you may recognize the following scenario. It goes something like this. You sowed $20 believing for 30, 60, or 100-fold in order to have enough finances to _____ (you fill in the blank). Later, you go to the grocery store where someone hands you $20. I've heard testimony after testimony of people who are pleased about this. Don't you know what just happened? **You just got your money back**. (Refer to Matthew 5:23 if necessary.)

Getting your money back proves that God is not mocked. Your seed was rejected. Your lukewarm offering just got spit out of God's mouth. If it was returned but not multiplied, God didn't *receive* it. If you gave $20 and got $20 right back, God didn't accept your gift. Where in the Bible did God ever **NOT** multiply something, but handed it back to the person who sowed it???

Why wasn't it *received*? Do you have ought against your brother? Does your brother have ought against you? Ex friend, ex-husband, ex-wife, Mother, father, sister, boss, child, aunt, uncle. Hate the pastor's wife? She knows it and so does God. You're probably the same type who loves their daddy and hated their mother. That's a demon, you know. First Lady is praying for you.

Was it a blemished offering? God hates all of that.

If you sowed $50 and only got back $20, chances are very good that the devourer got your refund before it could get back to you. After a few days or weeks when you get no harvest from that seed, you will need to check yourself and especially your tithing so that the devourer can be rebuked off of your returns.

Next, and immediately you need to check your lifestyle. Check for sin and attitudes to find out why your seeds are not being *received*.

When you do not sow properly, getting God's attention, the King of Glory cannot protect your harvest. The Lord of the Harvest cannot help you harvest a bounty, especially if you do not get God's attention in your sowing. You will not have His attention in the growing, and there will be no reaping.

> Be not deceived. God is not mocked, for whatsoever a man, soweth that shall he also reap, (Galatian 6:7).

We've always taken the above verse to mean that if a man sows nothing, he'll receive nothing. Or if a man sows wrong behavior toward his brother, he'll reap accordingly. It does mean all of that. But as it pertains to yourselves, seed or offering, it means that if a man sows fake worship, memorized prayers, and a stingy seed, he will reap accordingly. As I said before, if you don't get God's attention in your sowing and encourage Him in your praise, keep Him around with your worship--, then the money you put in the offering basket was just giving. Add that meaningless, unconnected action to your works. But if God didn't receive it, it wasn't a good work that will live, grow, and prosper to harvest.

Good News

What are you supposed to be doing in this place where God has *sent* you? Sharing the Gospel of the Good News of Jesus Christ. Know what you believe in and be ready to defend it. You don't just share verbally, but in deed and in action, you show Christ. If people don't even know if you're a Christian, or that you're a Christian, you need to step up your witness. No, you do not preach damnation, fire and brimstone to those you meet. You share the Gospel of Reconciliation. Share your testimony. Let people know that God is not holding anything against them and that they can come to Him.

Your Great commission is to share the Gospel wherever you are and wherever you've been sent or assigned, even if it is just to your neighbor across the street.

And this gospel of the kingdom shall be preached in all the world for a witness unto all nations then shall the end come, (Matthew 24:14)

For those who don't want the end to come, then you haven't read the Book that tells us that we win. For those who think they can manipulate when the end comes, no man knows the day nor the hour. But know this, if you don't do the work of an evangelist, if you don't preach Christ, and Him crucified, if you don't win souls, that will not stop Christ from coming. Someone else will do it and you will be accounted as evil and disobedient.

So for the sake of the Gospel, get to the tasks at hand, do the work of ministry, whatever you are called to do, and glorify God. Amen.

Did you know this?

Wisdom does.

Other books by this author

AK: The Adventures of the Agape Kid

AMONG SOME THIEVES

Ancestral Powers https://a.co/d/ikcxccC

Blindsided: *Has the Old Man Bewitched You?* https://a.co/d/5O2fLLR

Churchzilla, The Wanna-Be, Supposed-to-be Bride of Christ

Demons Hate Questions

Devil Weapons: Unforgiveness, Bitterness,… https://a.co/d/g2ghpmc

Dream Defilement https://a.co/d/gwBBnfU

Don't Refuse Me, Lord (series)

https://a.co/d/1yehbDv

Every Evil Bird

Evil Touch

Fantasy Spirit Spouse

FAT Demons (The): *Breaking Demonic Curses*

The Fold (5 book series)

- The Fold https://a.co/d/49nwpnI
- Name Your Seed https://a.co/d/4VxcXzo
- The Poor Attitudes of Money https://a.co/d/gObG7cx
- Do Not Orphan Your Seed https://a.co/d/5hGAbBP
- For the Sake of the Gospel (5)

My Sowing Journal is to keep up with seed sown.
https://a.co/d/1uXX54B

got HEALING? Verses for Life

got LOVE? Verses for Life

got HOPE? Verses for Life

got money?

How to Dental Assist

Let Me Have A Dollar's Worth

Living for the NOW of God

Lose My Location https://a.co/d/crD6mV9

Man Safari, *The*

Marriage Ed. *Rules of Engagement & Marriage*

Made Perfect in Love

Motherboard (The) - *Soul Prosperity Series*

Plantation Souls

Power Money: Nine Times the Tithe

https://a.co/d/629G7n7

The Power of Wealth *(forthcoming)*

Rules of Engagement & Marriage

Seasons of Grief

Seasons of War

Soul Prosperity https://a.co/d/5p8YvCN

Souls Captivity *-Soul Prosperity series 2*

The Spirit of Poverty https://a.co/d/blmZNFH

This Is NOT That: How to Keep Demons from Coming at You https://a.co/d/8XTnsIZ

Throne of Grace: Courtroom Prayer

Time Is of the Essence

Too Many Wives: *Why You Have Lady Problems*

Tormenting Spirits https://a.co/d/dAogEJf

Triangular Power *(series)*

    Powers Above

    SUNBLOCK

    Do Not Swear by the Moon

    STARSTRUCK

Upgrade: How to Get Out of Survival Mode, Toxic Souls (Book 2)

Legacy (Book 3

Warfare Prayer Against Beauty Curses

Warfare Prayer Against Poverty https://a.co/d/88SZXDx

When the Devourer is Rebuked

The Wilderness Romance *(series)*

- *The Social Wilderness*
- *The Sexual Wilderness*
- *The Spiritual Wilderness*

Dear Reader

Thank you for acquiring and reading this book. I pray that it and the series have taught you and blessed you tremendously.

God's Grace to you,

Dr. Marlene Miles

www.ingramcontent.com/pod-product-compliance
Lightning Source LLC
Chambersburg PA
CBHW070855050426
42453CB00012B/2216